Make Your Own...

Videos, Commercials, Radio Shows, Special Effects, and More

By The Fun Group
Illustrated by Ellen Sasaki

Published by Grosset & Dunlap, New York,
in association with Nickelodeon Books™

D1524031

Editorial services by Parachute Press, Inc.

Cover art by Gary Baseman
Book design by Michel Design

Library of Congress Catalog Card Number: 90-86409
ISBN: 0-448-40201-7
A   B   C   D   E   F   G   H   I   J

1
It's
Show Time

If you like watching Nickelodeon, you'll like reading this book! Why? Because it shows you how to turn your backyard, basement, neighborhood park—whatever—into a Nickelodeon home studio! You'll be able to produce, direct, and even star in your own shows—the Nick way!

Do you love *Double Dare*? Do you love *Make the Grade*? How would you like to host your own game show? Check out chapter 2. It has a step-by-step blueprint for creating your own game show. Some of the contestants answer trivia questions—and others do the dirty work! Chapter 2 even tells you how to build your own gooey, sticky obstacle course.

What's got vampires and space aliens in the school cafeteria? It's chapter 5, "Skit City." You can't do that on television, but you can do it at home! We'll help you put on the fastest, funniest skit show in the neighborhood.

Hey, dude—can you make up a TV sitcom that's as crazy as *Hey Dude*? Sure you can, when you read chapter 6. He's a kid. He's a dentist. He's Dr. Chuckie, D.D.S. It's a wild and crazy sitcom that you can put on yourself!

And speaking of neighborhoods, in chapter 7, Nick tells you how to shoot hilarious home videos. When you shoot these home videos, real life gets on tape. And who ever said real life can't be funny? It can be—and when it is, you'll be there to capture those hilarious moments.

Home videos! Sitcoms! Game shows! More! It's all here, with easy-to-follow instructions. There are scripts already written for you, plus tips on how to write your own.

So don't just watch Nickelodeon. Gather up some friends, get out there, and make your own!

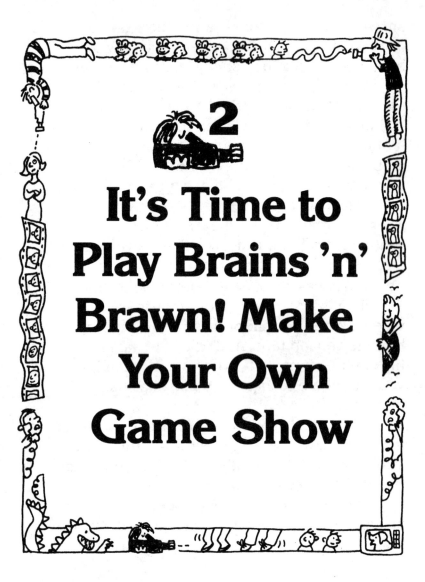

2
It's Time to Play Brains 'n' Brawn! Make Your Own Game Show

When it comes to game shows, Nickelodeon wins every time. Now you can get in on the fast and furious action with Brains 'n' Brawn—your own game show!

What You Need

- permission to turn your backyard, basement, or park into a game show arena
- 13 index cards
- a pen
- 2 bicycle helmets
- 2 bridge or card tables
- a big piece of posterboard
- a big felt-tip marker
- the Game Show Question Kit, and
- the Easy Obstacle Course Guide—found right in this book!

Brains 'n' Brawn, Phase 1: Question Central

Brains 'n' Brawn is a game that asks contestants to use their brains—and arms and legs—to win. First "the Brain" has to give correct answers to tough questions. Then "the Brawn" has to complete a messy physical stunt.

Choose 13 questions from the Game Show

Question Kit on pages 11-16. Write one question on each index card.

Whatever you do, don't write the answers on the index cards! The answers are for your eyes only, since you'll be acting as the host and running the show. Write the number of the question in the upper right-hand corner of the card. That way you'll be able to find the answer easily in the book.

Brains 'n' Brawn: The Setup

Place the two tables about 8 feet apart at one end of your backyard or basement. The members of each team will stand behind one of the tables. Make sure the area between the tables is clean—and free of stones, if you're playing outside.

You can decorate the tables to make them look cool. Put a sign that says "Brains 'n' Brawn Team 1" on one table and a sign that says "Brains 'n' Brawn Team 2" on the other.

Then make your Brains 'n' Brawn Official Scoreboard. Divide the posterboard into two columns. Write "Team 1" at the top of one column and "Team 2" at the top of the other. Use this to keep track of the score.

Brains 'n' Brawn: Playing the Game

You play this game with two-player teams— just like *Double Dare.* One player on each team will be the Brain, the one who answers the questions. The other will be the Brawn, the one who does the physical stunts. Before the players take their places behind the tables, have each team's Brawn put on a bicycle helmet.

As the host, you begin by throwing the

index cards into the area between the tables. Each Brawn scrambles to pick up as many cards as possible, and then gives them back to you. Whichever team has collected more cards goes first. You shuffle the 13 question cards and ask the first Brain a question. The Brain and Brawn of a team can talk to each other, but the Brain does all the talking for the team. Brawns do all the moving. If a Brawn answers for the team, the team loses 1 point and a turn.

Teams score 1 point per correct answer. Keep track of the score on your homemade scoreboard.

If Team 1 misses a question, for example, then Team 2 gets a chance to answer it. If Team 2 gets it right, that team gets 2 points! If Team 2 misses, Team 1 gets the next question and so on.

The Game Show Question Kit

Choose your questions from this list of super stumpers! The answers are on page 16.

1. What is Mr. Ed's owner's name?

2. True or False: Sneezes travel at over 100 miles per hour.

3. What is the only animal with four knees?

4. Who was the president of the United States during the Civil War?

5. People snore more in one season than they do in all the others. What season is that?

6. How many hours a day does the average American stay indoors?

7. True or False: It takes 750 gallons of paint to paint the White House.

8. True or False: Other than humans, pigs are the only mammals that get sunburned.

9. True or False: The longest major-league baseball game lasted 12 hours and 6 minutes.

10. True or False: Koalas are bears.

11. What are the names of the four presidents whose images are carved into Mount Rushmore?

12. Who invented the record player?

13. True or False: You can't burp when you lie on your back.

14. Name the head riding instructor on *Hey Dude.*

15. What color is a garnet?

16. What two teams did Bo Jackson play for at the same time?

17. If you were looking for it, where in your body would you find your medulla?

18. What is the name of the character Madonna played in *Dick Tracy*?

19. In the comic strip *Calvin and Hobbes*, who or what is Hobbes?

20. Which is not a real place?
   a. Hog Shooter, Oklahoma
   b. Cairo, Illinois
   c. Bedsprings, Iowa

21. What's the one thing that can kill Superman?

22. Which animal is not real?
   a. Tasmanian devil
   b. Duckbill platypus
   c. Five-toed furface

23. What is Inspector Gadget's favorite word?

24. What is the name of the first Mickey Mouse cartoon?
   a. "Steamboat Willie"
   b. "Steamboat Mickey"
   c. "Call Me Mickey!"

25. In the fairy tale "The Twelve Dancing Princesses," how does the king know his daughters are dancing all night?

26. In the movie *The Wizard of Oz,* what does the Wizard ask Dorothy to bring him?

27. Goofus and Gallant are two characters in *Highlights for Children* magazine. Which one is the good boy, and which one is the bad boy?

28. In what city and state are the Nickelodeon studios?

29. On *Looney Tunes,* who is always trying to hunt Bugs Bunny?

30. What breed of dog is Lassie?

31. True or False: The Baby Ruth candy bar was named after the famous baseball player Babe Ruth.

32. How do you kill a vampire?
    a. By throwing water on him
    b. By driving a stake through his heart
    c. By burning him at the stake

33. What animal does a cygnet grow up to be?

34. Name the Teenage Mutant Ninja Turtles.

35. What is the name of the dude ranch on *Hey Dude*?

36. If you suffer from arachnophobia, what are you afraid of?
a. Loud noises
b. Long words
c. Spiders

Answers:

1. Wilbur; **2.** True; **3.** An elephant; **4.** Abraham Lincoln; **5.** Summer; **6.** 17 hours; **7.** True; **8.** True; **9.** False; **10.** False; **11.** George Washington, Thomas Jefferson, Abraham Lincoln, and Theodore Roosevelt; **12.** Thomas Edison; **13.** True; **14.** Brad; **15.** Red; **16.** Kansas City Royals and Los Angeles Raiders; **17.** In your brain; **18.** Breathless Mahoney; **19.** A stuffed tiger; **20.** C; **21.** Green kryptonite; **22.** C; **23.** Wowser; **24.** A; **25.** Their new slippers are worn out every morning; **26.** The broomstick of the Wicked Witch of the West; **27.** Gallant is the good one, Goofus is the bad; **28.** Orlando, Florida; **29.** Elmer Fudd; **30.** Collie; **31.** False. It was named for President Grover Cleveland's oldest daughter; **32.** B; **33.** A swan; **34.** Donatello, Michelangelo, Raphael, Leonardo; **35.** Bar None; **36.** C.

The Obstacle Course Guide

Once the teams have completed all the questions, it's time for the Brawns to try the Obstacle Course. Before you start, set up all the equipment you'll need for your Obstacle Course.

Remember! Be sure you have permission from your parents to set up the Obstacle Course. Do it outside or someplace that you're allowed to mess up. Failure to comply with this warning could result in severe consequences —like being grounded for life!!!

You can set up your Obstacle Course in either of two ways: (1) Make two identical Obstacle Courses and have the Brawns race against each other at the same time, or (2) make only one course and time each Brawn as he or she goes through, one at a time. The faster time wins. Start with Obstacle #1 and then go on to #2, #3, and so on.

Obstacle #1: *Pop Pockets*

You need (per Obstacle Course): a pair of big, floppy pants; a chair; at least 6 small balloons; water

Before you start, fill the balloons with water. The Brawns have to put on the pants and carefully sit on a chair. No problem—except that the pants have water balloons in the back pockets! If a Brawn breaks a balloon, he or she must take off the pants and start again. If the balloons don't break, the Brawns take off the pants and run to . . .

Obstacle #2: *Cool Shoes*

You need big, old shoes; a big bowl full of wet sponges, cut up

Contestants must take off their shoes and socks and put on a pair of big, old, *squishy* shoes—squishy because they're filled with wet sponges! Then it's on to . . .

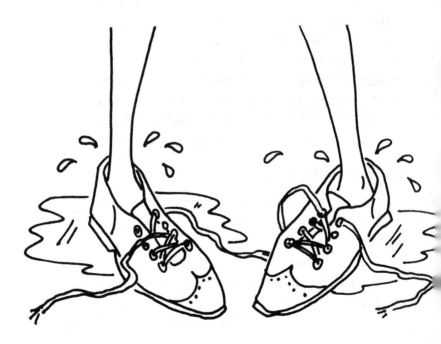

Obstacle #3: *Card Tricks*

You need a deck of playing cards; a Hula Hoop or some other kind of hoop

Contestants stand 3 feet from a Hula Hoop that's on the ground and carefully pitch cards into the hoop. When they get five inside the hoop, they're ready to move on to . . .

Obstacle #4: *Letter Perfect*

You need an envelope; a piece of paper; a pair of mittens

This one is so easy! All the contestants have to do is open an envelope and read a letter. Where's the challenge? Well, they have to put on the mittens first. When they get the letter open (finally!), they must take off the mittens and go to . . .

Obstacle #5: *Can't Touch This!*

You need a bag of marshmallows; an empty plastic bowl; a bowl of chocolate syrup

Dump the marshmallows into the syrup. Brawns must pick a marshmallow out of the bowl of chocolate syrup and spit it into the other bowl. Not too tough, but one more rule—no hands, please—not even when picking up the marshmallow! If a Brawn manages to get three marshmallows into the empty bowl, the game is over!

Give 10 points to the team that completed the Obstacle Course first or in the shorter amount of time. Now add the points earned by the Brains to the points earned by the Brawns. Whichever team has more points is the winner!

Brains 'n' Brawn is a great game for parties or anytime. You can play it more than once. Let the Brains change places with the Brawns. Change the rules; make up your own obstacles. Find new questions from trivia books. And, of course, you don't always have to be the host. There's only one rule in a Nickelodeon game show: Kids always win!

3
Rad Radio—
Make
Your Own
Radio Show

What if dinosaurs marched up your street and stepped on your neighbor's house? What if aliens showed up in your cafeteria for a food fight—and they brought their own food? You can make these things—and anything else you can think of—happen on WYOU, the radio station you control!

Since you're on radio, you don't need to *show* your audience any real action. You can "go" anywhere and "do" anything at all. You don't need expensive props. You don't even need costumes. All you need is imagination, a tape recorder, and a few Nick tricks!

You can spoof a news program or a soap opera, record your own commercials and funny stories—anything you want!

One of the best things about radio is the sound effects. You can make "walls" come crashing down just by chomping on a stalk of celery. Use the Handy Sound Effects Starter Kit in this chapter to add ear-boggling noises to your radio shows. Then, once you get the hang of those, you can make up your own ways of creating rad radio sounds.

Breaking the Sound Barrier

Years ago, before TV, radio plays were staged every day. Sound effects experts used various props to create the sounds that made scripts come alive. They had an actual car door to slam. They hit a big sheet of metal to make the sound of thunder.

Now it's your turn. You can easily make your own sound effects and put them together with the script on page 27 to produce an original radio play called *Tyrannosaurus Mess!* It's about the day a dinosaur turned a corner, came up a block, and squashed all the houses in a suburban neighborhood! Maybe yours!

Rehearse your radio play with the sound effects a few times to get the timing right. Then, when you're ready, turn on the tape recorder and record it.

The Handy Sound Effects Starter Kit

Every noise you need for *Tyrannosaurus Mess!* is here.

Rock 'n' roll music—Tune your radio to a station, wait for the right song, and start recording, or tape a favorite song from a CD or record.

Static—Scrape a butter knife over a piece of dry toast.

Person talking from far away—Hold your nose and talk.

People screaming—Get some friends to scream into the microphone.

Person running—Put your hands inside an empty pair of shoes and pound them quickly on a wooden board or table.

People running—Ask two friends to put their hands in some empty shoes and quickly pound on the wooden board together.

Dinosaur roar—Roar into a tall glass near the microphone.

Dinosaur footsteps—Slowly and heavily pound your fists on a wooden table.

Horses' hooves—Turn two plastic cups upside down and clap them on a wooden board.

Foghorn—Blow across the mouth of an empty large glass soda bottle or jug, near the microphone.

Mice squeaking—Rub your fingers over a wet balloon.

Thunder—Shake a big aluminum cookie sheet.

Rain—Drop uncooked rice onto a tin pie plate. The more rice you drop, the harder it will "rain."

Walls crashing down—Break or bite a stalk of celery near the microphone.

Clothes tearing—Rip a sheet or a rag near the microphone. (Be sure to get permission for this.)

Person falling—Drop a heavy book on a rug.

Giant grasshoppers hopping—Hold 4 inches of a metal ruler on a table with one hand. Let 8 inches hang over the side and twang the overhanging part with the other hand.

Tyrannosaurus Mess!— A Radio Script

The Cast

- Dr. Crazy, WYOU's rock 'n' roll deejay
- Sue Sneed, WYOU's news announcer
- Sam Sampson, WYOU's remote-news reporter
- Alice, a panicking citizen
- *Tyrannosaurus rex,* a dinosaur
- Police officer (on horseback)

Props

- an audiocassette recorder with a microphone (if it's not yours, be sure to ask the owner if it's okay to use it)
- a blank cassette
- a stalk of celery
- a tin pie plate
- some uncooked rice
- a heavy book
- a rug
- some friends
- 3 pairs of shoes—not sneakers, and preferably different kinds and sizes

- a tall glass
- an empty glass soda bottle or a jug
- a radio tuned to a rock station
- 3 wooden rulers
- a wooden table
- a piece of dry toast
- a butter knife
- 2 plastic cups
- a wooden board
- a wet balloon
- an aluminum cookie sheet
- an old bedsheet or rag you have permission to rip

Okay, now you're ready to rehearse.

The Script

SOUND EFFECT: THE LAST FEW BARS OF A ROCK 'N' ROLL SONG

Dr. Crazy: You're listening to WYOU—You Want It? You Got It—Radio! This is Dr. Crazy. My music show is insane! Wait a minute, folks. Something insane is happening right now! The red news light is flashing! It's Sue Sneed with what looks like an emergency news bulletin.

Sue Sneed: Thank you, Dr. Crazy! This just in—and some of you folks are not going to believe it! A *Tyrannosaurus rex* is headed for

_____!

(FILL IN THE NAME OF A STREET IN YOUR NEIGHBORHOOD)

No one knows where it came from, and no one knows where it's going! Let's go to our remote unit, where Sam Sampson is standing by with a live report. Sam? Are you there?

SOUND EFFECT: STATIC

Sam Sampson (sounding as if from far away): It's panic city here, Sue! We're about three blocks ahead of the giant lizard, and everyone's leaving home!

SOUND EFFECT: PEOPLE RUNNING AND SCREAMING

Sam: Slow down! Wait! Say a word to the folks over the radio! You! Stop! What's your name?

Alice (panting): Alice! Wow! WYOU! My favorite radio station! I'm wearing your T-shirt, see? But I can't stop now! There's a dinosaur coming and I've got to go! Rock on!

SOUND EFFECT: PERSON RUNNING

Sam: Well, Sue, you heard it here. Let's try to get a little closer! That is, if we don't get crushed! Wait! What's that?

SOUND EFFECT: DINOSAUR ROAR

Sam: That's him! That's him! I can see him now over the top of that office building! Ooh! He's a big one!

SOUND EFFECT: DINOSAUR FOOTSTEPS (CONTINUOUSLY FROM THIS POINT ON, THE DINOSAUR'S FOOTSTEPS AND ROAR CAN BE HEARD IN THE BACKGROUND)

Sam: Can you hear him? Oh, this is truly terrifying! This is worse than King Kong! Where's the army? Where are the police?

SOUND EFFECT: HORSES' HOOVES
Police officer (ON HORSEBACK): Whoa! Whoa, girl!
Sam: You're a police officer! Are you going to help stop the *Tyrannosaurus*?
Police officer: Are you kidding? We always get our criminal, but no one said anything about getting our dinosaur! We're out of here!

SOUND EFFECT: HORSES' HOOVES
Sam: Oh! Who will help? Who?

SOUND EFFECT: FOGHORN
Sam: Hooray! It's the navy! But wait! They're running away, too. And now it looks like, yes, I'm right, even the mice are leaving!

SOUND EFFECT: MICE SQUEAKING
Sam: Go on, you mice! Scram!

SOUND EFFECTS: THUNDER AND RAIN
Sam: Oh, no! Now it's raining! It's a bad day on

_____ ! (NAME OF STREET)
The dinosaur is headed straight for number
_____! No!

SOUND EFFECT: WALLS CRASHING DOWN
Sam: The dinosaur is taking out a whole block of houses! This is terrible! Now he's reaching

down for me! Oh, no! How will I ever escape?

SOUND EFFECTS: CLOTHING (OLD BEDSHEET) TEARING, PERSON FALLING

Sam: Destruction is everywhere! They're going to have to contact the President on his golf course! The President is going to have to declare this neighborhood a disaster area!

SOUND EFFECT: GIANT GRASSHOPPERS HOPPING

Sam: What's that? It looks like a cloud jumping up and down.

SOUND EFFECT: GIANT GRASSHOPPERS HOPPING

Sam: It can't be! But it is! Giant grasshoppers are hopping down the street by the thousands!

SOUND EFFECT: GIANT GRASSHOPPERS HOPPING

Sam: I'm getting out of here, Sue! In fact, I quit! Get someone else to do these live remote reports for WYOU—You Want It! You Got It!— Radio!

SOUND EFFECTS: PERSON RUNNING, STATIC

Sue: Thank you, Sam. And now back to Dr. Crazy!
Dr. Crazy: That was wild! And it just proves that anything you can think of can happen on WYOU, the radio station you control! And now let's hear some more rockin' rock 'n' roll!

SOUND EFFECT: ROCK 'N' ROLL MUSIC

THE END

Whew! Now that the dinosaur is gone, it's your turn. Make your own radio script. The best scripts have lots of opportunities for sound effects. Experiment with new sound effects. It's your turn to sound off!

4

Music Video City— Make Your Own Music Video

Want to make your own music video? It's a great way to experiment with your favorite songs and your weirdest ideas. All you need is some music, some kids, and a video camera, and you're off! You can do anything you want!

But what if you're not quite sure how to start? Don't worry! Try this Do-It-Yourself Music Video System and get ready to pump it up!

How It Works

The Do-It-Yourself Music Video System tells you how to put together a great music video. You can follow the scene-by-scene breakdown, or change it in any way you like. And in slightly more time than you can say "Nick Rocks," you'll be inviting your friends over for a private playback!

You don't need a copy of the latest hit song to make a cool music video. With a little imagination, you can use *anything*! Here's a tune that everybody knows—"I've Been Working on the Railroad"—but by changing the words a little, you can turn it into your own video!

Important: Before you begin, be sure to get permission to use the camera and to shoot your video in the kitchen, the playroom, the backyard, the park, and anywhere else you plan to be. If you're not comfortable using the video camera—or if the owner of the camera doesn't want you to use it, just make him or her the camera person. Then you get to be the director, in other words, the boss. That's the way it's done in Hollywood.

What You Need

- a video camera
- an audiocassette recorder
- an audiocassette of the song "I've Been Working on the Railroad" (with Nickelodeon words; see below) which you and your friends have recorded in advance

Props

- thick textbooks
- notebooks
- pens
- a piece of chalk
- a blackboard (if you have one)
- straight-backed chairs
- a lawn chair
- a newspaper
- some glasses of lemonade or other cool drink
- a plant sprayer
- rakes and gardening tools
- dirty dishes and pots
- a dishcloth
- dishwashing liquid
- aprons
- a bucket
- 3 sponges or mops

You also need: 4 friends to sing lip-synch, 3 more friends to act as extras, and 3 grown-ups

Note: Don't worry if you can't round up seven kids; any number can play. And if you can't get grown-ups to play the grown-up parts, you can use kids.

Your actors can sing live on the video—or they can do it the way most rock video stars do it. They can lip synch. Just record the gang singing this special version of "I've Been Working on the Railroad." Then let the actors lip synch to it.

How to Lip-Synch: Lip-synching means mouthing the words to a song instead of actually singing it. It's easy to do. Just place your audiocassette player about 6 inches from the microphone on your video camera and play the song you want to lip-synch to. Then have your lip-synchers mouth the words in time to the music. But make sure they practice first—it can be tricky to get the timing just right. And remember, any noises they make will come out in your video.

The Song

Here are the complete lyrics to the Nick version of "I've Been Working on the Railroad."

I've been working on my homework
All the live long day.
I've been working on my homework
And I've got no time to play.
Don't you hear the alarm clock clanging
Rise up so early in the dawn
Can't you hear the teacher shouting,
"Children rake the lawn!"
Children won't you rake
Children won't you rake
Children won't you rake the
lawn, lawn, lawn.
Children won't you rake
Children won't you rake
"Children won't you rake the lawn."
Someone's in the kitchen doing dishes
Someone's in the kitchen I know-o-o
Someone's in the kitchen doing dishes
And scrubbing on the old floor-o.
Fee-fi-fiddly -i-o
Fee-fi-fiddly -i-o
Fee-fi-fiddly -i-o
Raking on the old lawn-o.

Scene 1: The Playroom

The Cast:

- teacher
- 3 friends
- 4 singers

The Setup

Sit 3 of your friends in the straight-backed chairs. Give them each a thick textbook, a notebook, and a pen. Hang a blackboard on one wall. (If you don't have a backboard, use a big sheet of cardboard.) Write on the blackboard:

Homework
- Read 25 chapters.
- Write 4 term papers.
- Do every math problem in the textbook.
- Don't go out.
- Don't have fun.

Ask a grown-up or whoever is playing the teacher to stand near the blackboard and hold a piece of chalk. Turn off the lights.

Action

It's totally dark. A flashlight switches on, shining straight up from under the face of the teacher. He or she says: "Now read chapters two through twenty-five..."

The room lights come on. Three kids sit on chairs. The teacher continues and taps his or her chalk on the blackboard.

". . . tonight and answer the questions at the end of each chapter. Your term papers are due in two days. Don't forget to type them."

The four singers appear. They carry notebooks and thick textbooks. They start lip-synching the first verse and chorus.

> I've been working on my homework
> All the live long day.
> I've been working on my homework
> And I've got no time to play.
> Don't you hear the alarm clock clanging
> Rise up so early in the dawn
> Can't you hear the teacher shouting,
> "Children . . ." (in teacher's voice)

After the singers sing the word "Children," the teacher will disappear and turn into the grown-up in the next scene. (To find out how to make your teacher disappear, turn to page 48.)

Scene 2: The Backyard

The Cast

- Parent
- 3 rakers
- 4 singers

The Setup

One friend rakes the lawn. Two others dig with gardening tools. Spray them with the plant sprayer so it looks as if they're sweating. A grown-up (or a kid playing one) relaxes on a lawn chair, holding the paper and drinking a lemonade.

Action

Start by making your grown-up appear in the classroom. You want it to look as if the teacher has turned into the grown-up, so place the grown-up in exactly the same spot where the teacher stood in the last scene. The singers sing the first line of the second verse: "Rake the lawn!" Then you cut to the backyard. The camera zooms in for a close-up of the cool, tall glass of lemonade. (See page 47 for how to use the zoom function on the camera.) A hand comes in and picks it up. Zoom out to show the grown-up sipping the lemonade and lounging on the lawn chair while the three lawn workers sweat in the background. The grown-up says:

"Now I want this lawn weeded and raked by five tonight. We're expecting company and the place has to look good. And don't forget to trim the edges."

The singers join the other kids and finish the second chorus.

"...rake the lawn!"
Children won't you rake
Children won't you rake
Children won't you rake the lawn,
lawn, lawn
Children won't you rake
Children won't you rake
"Children won't you rake the lawn."

At the end of this verse, they disappear.

Scene 3: The Kitchen

The Cast

- a mom
- 4 singers
- 3 floor-scrubbers

The Setup

Pile the pots and dirty dishes in the sink. Fill the sink with soapy water.

Action

Focus your camera on a close-up of the dirty dishes. Then zoom out to show the four singers at the sink. They wear aprons. The other kids are scrubbing the floor. A grown-up (or kid) playing a mom comes in and says:

"Now I expect those dishes to be done when I come home. And when you finish, don't forget the bathroom, den, and your bedroom."

When she leaves, turn on the music tape. When the music starts, the group starts washing dishes and lip-synching the third chorus.

Someone's in the kitchen doing dishes
Someone's in the kitchen I know-o-o-o
Someone's in the kitchen doing dishes
And scrubbing on the old floor-o.

43

At the end of the third chorus, the singers walk toward the mom. She looks scared.

Scene 4: The Backyard

The Cast

- 3 grown-ups
- 4 singers
- the rest of the kids

The Setup

The grown-ups hold rakes and gardening tools. They're all sweating. The singers and the rest of the kids sit on and around the lounge chair. Each has a tall glass of lemonade.

Action

Focus your camera on a close-up of a rake. Then zoom out to show the grown-ups working on the lawn as the kids relax on the lounge chairs. The kids sing the fourth verse. Just before the last line, they say,
    "And don't forget to trim the edges!"
They laugh and finish the song.

Fee-fi-fiddly-i-o
Fee-fi-fiddly-i-o-o-o-o
Fee-fi-fiddly-i-o--
"And don't forget to trim the edges!"
Raking on the old lawn-o!

THE END

Does this script give you ideas for making your own video? You don't have to make your video exactly like this. You can change the script in any way to make it work best for you.

Bonus Extra— Special Effects

Put your creative touch on your music video! Read through the following special effects and try out the ones that will make your tape totally cool!

Lights

You can do a lot with a little lighting. For normal-looking daytime lighting, place a light to the side of your camera and slightly above it. Aim it at your performers. This will give your video a more professional look.

Flashlight—With the rest of the lights off, shine the flashlight straight up under your star's chin for a thriller effect. Or turn it on and off rapidly for a strobelike effect. (This works only in a dark room.)

Use the flashlight to make a light show behind your rock star. Shine the flashlight at a large sheet of foil, and aim the foil at your star. Move the foil, and light patterns will shimmer on the wall behind the star.

Candlelight—Great for letter-writing scenes and late-night scenes. Candles look streaky on video.

Car headlights—Great for outdoor shots. Shine them at a wall and they're great for shadow shots. (Have an adult turn them on for you.)

Video Effects

You don't need to buy a million-dollar electronic system to put some superspecial effects into your music video. Some good old creative thinking—plus the special controls built into the video camera—can make you a special effects wizard.

Note: Most of these effects work best if you put your camera on a tripod or other steady surface. This keeps your picture from looking wobbly.

Who's Zooming Who?

Ever see a video where the subject is far away, and then the camera starts to move in until suddenly the subject's face fills the whole screen? That's called zooming in. A zoom shot is controlled by a zoom button on your video camera. You push the button while you're shooting, and the camera automatically zooms in.

You can also zoom out. Start on a close-up of a photograph or the telephone and push the zoom-out button to move away from it. Or try a bouncing shot—zoom out, zoom in, and zoom out again.

Panning

Technically, "panning" means moving the camera from one scene to another while shooting. You can pan up from an object to your star's face. You can pan down from the top of a tree to its roots.

If you pan very quickly, you can blur the scene.

Head over Heels

Make your rock stars dance on the ceiling. No special shoes or rigging is necessary. Just turn the camera upside down and shoot!

Earthquake!

Shake the camera gently to make the scene appear as if it were rocking. (Add sound effects from chapter 3 for added realism.)

Disappearing Act

Your rock stars can start out singing in the bathroom and then suddenly vanish and reappear on the sidewalk. How? Through fingertip on/off action.

Set up your shot in the bathroom. Shoot your singers while they lip-synch the part of the song you want sung in the bathroom. When you want the disappearing act to begin, push the pause button (*not* the off button) on the camera. Have the singers rush out of the bathroom. Keep your viewfinder focused on the exact spot they were in. When the singers are gone, turn the camera on again (press the pause button) and shoot that same spot for a few seconds more. Be very careful not to move the camera or anything else in the picture during this shot. Only your singers should move.

Turn off the camera and take your singers outside. Shoot the exact spot where you want your singers to appear—*without* your singers. Then push the pause button and don't move the camera. (A tripod will really help here.) Bring the singers in and push the pause button again to restart the taping. When you watch the videotape, it will look almost as if your singers had popped into the scene.

Tints and Textures

You can change the color and feeling of your scenes by shooting through different materials.

Colored cellophane—Attach a piece of colored cellophane to the front of your lens with a piece of tape and turn your scenes yellow, blue, green, or red—according to the color of the cellophane.

Fishnet or gauze—Wrap a piece of either material around your lens. The tiny diamonds and squares in these materials will smooth the edges of whatever you're shooting and give a soft, romantic feel.

A plastic bag—Clear plastic over the lens will make your shot look cloudy.

A glass of water—Water will change the size and shape of your subject. Find a glass or bowl that's wider than your lens and fill it with water. Have an assistant hold it just in front of the camera while you shoot through it. Your performers will look as if they were in a fun-house mirror!

A spoon—Find a big, shiny spoon. Hold it so that your star's face is reflected in it. Zoom the camera in on the reflection. Then pan up to your star's real face.

The Rap Factor

Rappin's a way for you to go
When you do your music video show
It's hot. It's hip. And that ain't jive!
Rap is rad—on tape or live!

For a rap no one can touch, have a friend provide a catchy beat by clapping, beating a drum, or making sounds with his or her mouth. Or just make the beat yourself and record it on an audiocassette. Then write your rap song to go with the beat. Rhyming isn't as hard as it seems, but while you're getting the hang of it, try rapping out some nursery rhymes or other poems. Once you get the rhythm down pat, you'll find it easier to make your own raps. It may take some time to find the right rhymes and some practice to get the rap to work in time with the beat. But before long you'll have a rap song good enough to shoot on video, perform live, or record on tape.

In the meantime, here's a rap you can personalize to suit yourself!

My name is _____
and I'm here to say
I'm the coolest kid on the block today.
My friends _____ and _____
are also cool.
We run it all at the _____
school.
And when we rap, we're really def
So move over Hammer, cool it Jeff.
Make room for the kids from _____
street.
As rappers and dancers we can't be beat!

5

Skit City– Make Your Own Funny Skits

You don't have to put on a big production to have a good time. Sometimes the simplest ideas are the funniest! Just get together with a few friends, add a few simple props, and you're ready to act up!

Skits should be short and funny. Think of a funny situation, such as a monster movie, a dumb commercial, or a mishap at lunch in the school cafeteria. Then get some kids together and let everyone chip in with ideas. Before long you'll be laughing and your skit will be practically written.

To get started, here are a few ready-made skits you can try.

Skit #1: Cafeteria Caper

The Cast

- Klagg and Frazz, 2 aliens
- Andrew, a student
- Suzanne, a student
- extra students, if possible

Props

- a table
- 2 cafeteria trays
- some food—your choice—on plates
- 2 chairs
- 4 plastic or paper straws
- some makeup (ask permission first)

The Setup

Arrange the table and chairs as if they were in your school cafeteria. If you have more than

four actors, have the "extras" sit at the table and pretend to eat. Leave two empty chairs side by side.

Choose two kids to be aliens. Tape two straws to the back of each one's head to look like antennas. Put makeup on their faces to make them look weird. Keep these two actors out of sight until it's time for them to come onstage.

Give the two cafeteria trays, with food on them, to the actors playing Andrew and Suzanne.

The Script

SUZANNE STANDS NEAR ONE OF THE TABLES LOOKING AROUND THE "CAFETERIA." ANDREW ENTERS.

Suzanne: Where have you been? I've been waiting for such a long time.

Andrew: I was standing in line behind Butch. He's the only person I know who really likes cafeteria food.

Suzanne: Well, I found two seats. Let's sit over there.

Andrew: Ten-four.

THEY SIT DOWN IN TWO EMPTY SEATS.

Suzanne: Doesn't this look awful?

56

Andrew: Gross. What is it supposed to be?

Suzanne: The menu said it was macaroni and cheese.

Andrew: It looks like alien food to me.

Suzanne: Even aliens wouldn't eat this.

KLAGG AND FRAZZ, THE ALIENS, WALK IN AND TAKE SUZANNE'S AND ANDREW'S PLATES RIGHT OFF THEIR TRAYS.

Klagg: Yes we would.

Frazz: Mmmm. My favorite.

THEY WALK OFF WITH THE PLATES.

OFFICIAL
WARNING
STOP!
DO NOT
GO ON!

We interrupt this book for a special announcement. Please ignore the script on the next three pages. This script is gross, disgusting . . . and our personal favorite.

Quick, turn the page!

Skit #2: Gross Out!

The Cast

- Kid #1
- Kid #2
- Kid #3

Props

- a can of cream of mushroom soup
- a soup spoon
- a large bowl
- 3 chairs

The Setup

Arrange the chairs in a row as if they were seats in a movie theater. Have the three kids sit next to each other. Kid #3 should put the bowl in his or her lap.

Open the can of mushroom soup. (Ask a grown-up to help with the can opener.)

Have Kid #3 hide the can carefully inside his or her shirt or jacket.

The Script

Kid #1: This is a great movie!

Kid #2: Yeah! I only wish I had enough money to buy something to eat!

Kid #3: Oh, don't mention food! I'm going to be sick!

KID #3 MAKES GAGGING NOISES, BENDS FORWARD AT THE WAIST AND SPILLS THE SOUP OUT INTO THE BOWL IN HIS OR HER LAP AS IF THROWING UP. KID #2 PULLS OUT A SPOON AND STARTS EATING THE SOUP.

Kid #2: Yum! I wanted popcorn but this will do!

THE END

Skit #3: The Operation

The Cast

- Doctor #1
- Doctor #2
- Patient

Props

- a long table
- 2 white bed sheets
- 2 ladders, five feet long
- a bright light
- a butter knife
- a clean plunger
- a knitting needle

Stuff to pull out of the patient* such as:
- a long piece of rope
- a bicycle tire
- a pair of boxer shorts
- some loose change
- an audiocassette
- a tape player
- a big soup pot

The Setup

Stretch one bed sheet between the two ladders, like a curtain. Place the bright light about 5 feet behind the sheet so it shines right into the sheet, toward the audience. Place the table behind the sheet and in front of the light. The audience won't see the table itself, only the shadow it casts on the sheet.

Drape the other sheet over the table like a tablecloth so it touches the ground. Put the junk you've collected under the sheet.

Have the patient lie down on the table. Have the two doctors stand between the table and the bright lamp.

---

*The idea is to look as if you're pulling all kinds of weird objects out of the patient, so use anything you can find!

The light casts shadows of the actors and the props on the sheet. The audience will see only the shadows. Be sure to speak loudly and clearly so that everyone can hear you from behind the sheet.

The Script

Patient: Gee, I hope you can help me. My stomach is killing me!

Doctor #1: We'll do what we can.

Doctor #2: Now go to sleep.

DOCTOR #1 PUTS THE PLUNGER NEAR THE PATIENT'S FACE FOR A SECOND. (DON'T ACTUALLY PUT IT ON ANYONE'S FACE—YUCK!)

Doctor #1: This is a difficult case.

Doctor #2: I know. Scalpel.

DOCTOR #1 HANDS DOCTOR #2 THE SCALPEL [BUTTER KNIFE]. DOCTOR #2 PRETENDS TO CUT THE PATIENT OPEN.

Doctor #2: Oh my gosh! Look at this!

DOCTOR #2 PULLS THE BICYCLE TIRE FROM UNDER THE SHEET, MAKING IT LOOK AS IF IT'S COMING OUT OF THE PATIENT. THE DOCTORS PULL OUT ALL THE PROPS ONE BY ONE, EXCLAIMING OVER EACH AND PULLING OUT THE ROPE, HAND OVER HAND. THE BIG SOUP POT IS TIED TO THE END. THE DOCTORS DANGLE IT OVER THE PATIENT FOR A SECOND, AND THEN PUT IT DOWN.

Doctor #1: Looks like that's everything. Let's sew him [OR HER] up.

DOCTOR #1 TAKES THE KNITTING NEEDLE AND PRETENDS TO SEW THE PATIENT UP. THE PATIENT SITS UP.

Patient: Gee! My stomachache's all gone! I feel better already!

Doctors #1 and #2: Wait until you get our bill!

THE END

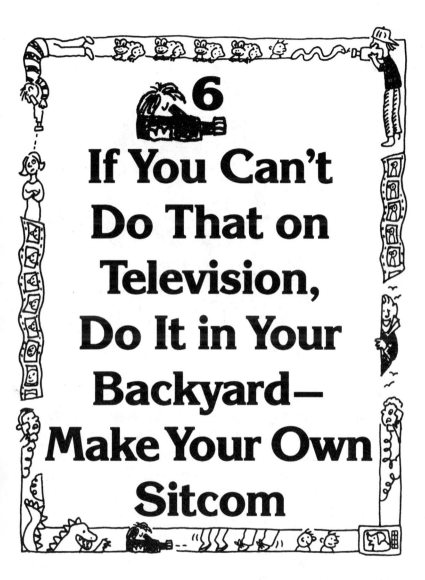

6

If You Can't Do That on Television, Do It in Your Backyard— Make Your Own Sitcom

Don't touch that dial! It's time for you to put on your own funny prime-time situation comedy starring you and your friends! You don't even need a video camera to put on a half-hour of wacky jokes and wild situations. You can do it live in front of a studio audience! Start with the script here, "Dr. Chuckie, D.D.S." Then make up new episodes or write your own.

Dr. Chuckie, D.D.S.

"Dr. Chuckie, D.D.S." is about the life and loves of a fourteen-year-old dentist who sets up his practice in the basement of his parents' house. He's old enough to drill teeth and fill cavities, but he's too young to drive a car.

The Cast

• Chuckie Brown, a cute fourteen-year-old genius who graduated from dental school early and set up his own practice in his parents' basement.

• Mrs. Mona Williams, Chuckie's assistant and receptionist. She tries to improve Chuckie's eating habits and wants him to act like a grown-up even though he's still a teen.

• Ginger Edwards, 14, cute, and Chuckie's ex-girlfriend. Sometimes Chuckie carves her initials on a filling.

Props

• a bottle of mouthwash
• a small chair
• a small table
• some small paper cups
• a package of green soft-drink mix
• some cotton
• a metal bowl
• a pencil (preferably a mechanical

pencil—the kind you fill with leads)
- a squirt gun
- some old wire
- a big flashlight (the bigger the better!)
- a big hand mirror
- a big white shirt
- a paper towel
- a turkey baster
- some 35mm slides
- some string

Note: It's not necessary to have all the props listed here, just whatever you think will make your set look like a dentist's office.

Now it's time to put together the set. The chair is Dr. Chuckie's dentist's chair. Place it in the center of the stage area. Place the small table to its left.

Attach the old wire to the eraser end of the pencil with some tape. Attach the other end of the wire to the underside of the small table. This is Dr. Chuckie's drill.

Attach more wire to the end of the squirt gun with some tape. Attach the other end to the underside of the table. This is Dr. Chuckie's water sprayer.

Punch two holes in the paper towel. Thread the piece of string through each hole and tie a knot at each end. Make sure it is long enough to hang around a person's neck. This is Dr.

Chuckie's drool napkin.

Place the paper cups on the table next to the metal bowl. This is Dr. Chuckie's spit sink. Place the cotton and mouthwash on the table, too. If you want, add some other metal tools to make it look more like a dentist's office.

The turkey baster is Dr. Chuckie's novocaine needle. Keep it hidden under the table until you need it. Put the slides under the table, too.

The white shirt is Dr. Chuckie's dental uniform. He wears it all the time.

The Script

Act 1: Dr. Chuckie's office

Dr. Chuckie: Ahh! The end of a hard day! Time for a soft drink!

DR. CHUCKIE POURS GREEN SOFT-DRINK POWDER INTO ONE OF HIS OFFICE PAPER CUPS AND FILLS IT UP WITH HIS WATER SPRAYER. HE LIFTS THE CUP TO MAKE A TOAST.

Dr. Chuckie: Here's fluoride in your eyeteeth!

AS HE LIFTS THE CUP TO HIS LIPS, MRS. WILLIAMS SWEEPS IN AND TAKES IT FROM HIS HAND.

Mrs. Williams: Grow up! Dentists don't drink this junk!

Dr. Chuckie: Come on, Mona. I'm a teenager.

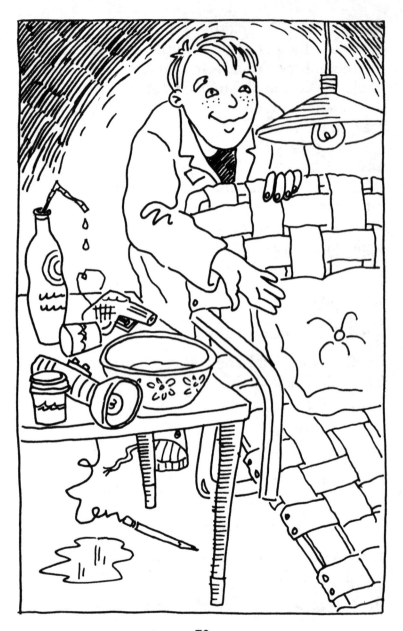

Mrs. Williams: You're a dentist. Act like one.

Dr. Chuckie: Give me a break! It's the end of the day.

Mrs. Williams: Not for you.

Dr. Chuckie: What do you mean?

Mrs. Williams: There's an emergency patient in the waiting room.

Dr. Chuckie: But me and the guys were going to shoot some hoops.

Mrs. Williams: Looks like you'll have to shoot some novocaine first, Doctor.

SHE CRACKS UP AT HER OWN JOKE.

Dr. Chuckie (SIGHING): Send the patient in.

MRS. WILLIAMS EXITS. CHUCKIE TURNS TO WASH HIS HANDS. AFTER A SECOND, GINGER ENTERS. BECAUSE HIS BACK IS TO THE DOOR, HE DOESN'T SEE HER COME IN.

Dr. Chuckie: Please sit down. I'll be with you in a minute.

HE POINTS TO THE DENTIST'S CHAIR WITHOUT TURNING AROUND.

Ginger: OK, Dr. Chuckie.

Dr. Chuckie: That voice! I'd know it anywhere!

HE TURNS AROUND.

Dr. Chuckie: Ginger-vitis!*

Ginger: Don't call me "Ginger-vitis"! That was one of the things that made me break up with you. None of my other boyfriends call me names that mean gum disease!

Dr. Chuckie: Why are you here—other than to tell me that you want me back forever?

Ginger (ROLLING HER EYES): I broke a tooth while eating a frozen candy bar.

HE PUTS A DROOL NAPKIN AROUND HER NECK.

Dr. Chuckie: Tsk, tsk, tsk. Who got you started on such a bad habit?

Ginger: You did.

Dr. Chuckie: Let's take a look at your tooth, okay? Open wide.

GINGER OPENS HER MOUTH. HE LOOKS INTO IT WITH A HUGE FLASHLIGHT AND A BIG MIRROR.

Dr. Chuckie: I see it. It's number thirteen. You broke your filling. It's too bad. You always had the most beautiful number thirteen tooth I ever saw. I'll have to drill.

HE BRINGS OUT HIS NEEDLE OF NOVOCAINE AND STANDS POISED TO SHOOT. HE PRETENDS TO PUT LOTS OF STUFF INTO HER MOUTH.

*Gingivitis is an inflammation of the gums.

Dr. Chuckie: So, you want to go out with me again?

Ginger: Mff, mff, mff.

Dr. Chuckie: Great. I'll pick you up at eight.

Act 2: Dr. Chuckie's office
It's dark. We hear voices.

Dr. Chuckie: Wasn't that movie great?

THE LIGHTS GO ON. DR. CHUCKIE AND GINGER ENTER.

Ginger: Well, it was bloody!

Dr. Chuckie: So's *Nightmare on Elm Street.*

Ginger: Yeah, but *Nightmare on Elm Street* has Freddie. This movie just has dentists drilling teeth.

Dr. Chuckie: Think of it as *Nightmare on Gum Street.* Want some Tutti Fruity Punch?

HE POURS PUNCH POWDER INTO TWO PAPER CUPS, TWIRLS THE SQUIRT GUN ON HIS FINGER, AND FILLS THE CUPS. HE HANDS ONE TO GINGER. THEY DRINK. HE TAKES HIS X RAYS (THE SLIDES) AND HOLDS THEM UP TO THE LIGHT.

Dr. Chuckie: There's something I have to show you. This is Milt the Stilt's mouth.

Ginger: You do Milt the Stilt's mouth?

Dr. Chuckie: I do.

Ginger: He's the best player on our basketball team. He shoots seventy points per game. He's the top man in the key.

Dr. Chuckie: He's the top man in decay, too. His teeth are a mess. Anyway, look at this. What do you see?

SHE LOOKS CLOSELY AT THE SLIDE.

Ginger: I see you on the beach with Marla Jacobs!

Dr. Chuckie: Let me see that!

HE GRABS THE SLIDE AWAY.

Dr. Chuckie: Oooops! Wrong slide! That was from last summer's vacation!

HE SHUFFLES THROUGH THE SLIDES QUICKLY AND HANDS ANOTHER TO GINGER.

Dr. Chuckie: Take a look at this one!

Ginger: Is it the Grand Canyon?

Dr. Chuckie: Nope. It's Milt's cavity.

HE HANDS HER A THIRD SLIDE.

Dr. Chuckie: This is after I filled it. What do you see?

Ginger: I see a heart and the initials "G.E." My initials—how sweet!

Dr. Chuckie: I also carved your initials in the principal's mouth.

Ginger: Not Dr. Mayhew!

Dr. Chuckie: Yep. You're in mouths all over town!

SHE LAUGHS.

Dr. Chuckie: Why did we break up?

Ginger: I guess root canals and romance just don't mix. All you care about is my teeth!

HE LEANS OVER AS IF HE WANTS TO KISS HER, THEN SUDDENLY SPOTS SOMETHING IN HER MOUTH. HE PULLS BACK AND GRABS THE TURKEY BASTER, MIRROR, ETC.

Dr. Chuckie: Wait. I think I missed something.

Ginger: You sure did!

SHE PICKS UP THE SQUIRT GUN AND SQUIRTS HIM IN THE FACE.

THE END

Want to write your own sitcom? Do it! Nick is here to help. Graham Yost, the head writer for *Hey Dude*, has some serious advice about how to write funny.

But first, take a look at some of Graham's work. Here is a funny scene from *Hey Dude* that you can also act out with your friends.

1. Exterior front of lodge

ERNST'S JEEP IS PARKED OUT FRONT. TED, BRAD, DANNY, AND MELODY WALK UP.

Danny: What does Mr. E want to see us about?

Ted: I don't know. But the jeep's out.

Melody: Maybe he's going on a trip.

THEY HEAR SOMEONE STUMBLE AND FALL. THEY LOOK AND SEE BUDDY SPRAWLED ON THE PATH IN FRONT OF THE LODGE, COMPUTER PRINTOUT PAPER STREWN OUT IN FRONT OF HIM.

Ted: Speaking of which. Hey, Bud-man, have a nice trip?

Danny: See you next fall.

Brad (TO TED AND DANNY): Get a life.

THE KIDS HURRY OVER TO BUDDY AND HELP HIM GATHER UP THE PAPER. BUDDY LOOKS DISTRAUGHT, LIKE HE'S SEEN A GHOST.

Buddy: Oh no. This is horrible.

Melody: Buddy, it's just paper. It didn't even tear. (GETS PAPER STACKED.) See? There. All better.

Buddy: Not that. (HEAD IN HANDS, MOANS.) It's a nightmare!

Brad: Buddy, what's wrong?

Buddy: I just had an idea for how the Bar None could make lots of money.

Ted: What's so scary about that?

Danny: Yeah. That's not a nightmare. Nightmares involve guys with razors for fingers.

Buddy: Wait till you hear the idea: We sell empty cans with labels on them saying, "The Original Bar None Allergy Cure—Pure Arizona Air." Isn't that horrifying?

Ted: What's so horrifying about that?

Melody: Buddy, it just sounds like one of your father's ideas.

Buddy: Exactly! That's what's so terrifying! I think I'm starting to become like him.

Writing Advice from Graham Yost

About the Characters

"The secret of success in any sitcom is having a good sense of who the characters are. In *Hey Dude*, it's the interplay between Ted, who's a jerk; Danny, who's straightforward; Melody, who's nice; Brad, who's rich; and Mr. Ernst, who's a nerd. When you create your characters, make them exaggerated versions of people you know. If your brother's a slob, make a character who's a *real* slob. But don't go too far. Keep the characters realistic—people respond to characters they can identify with."

The Setting

"For a good sitcom, you need a situation that has lots of variety that you can turn to again and again, and that you can bring people in and out of. The situation in *Perfect Strangers* is two cousins—one a foreigner—sharing an apartment. In *Hey Dude,* the situation is teenagers working at the Bar None, a dude ranch. The Bar None is a great setting for a sitcom because people can come and go."

Making It Funny

"Much of *Hey Dude*'s comedy is physical humor—Ted falling into a water trough, Brad and Ted getting handcuffed together, Mr. Ernst bumping his head. With a really good joke, the setup makes you think you're going in one direction and then the punchline is a surprise. The reason this scene from *Hey Dude* is funny is because we don't know why Buddy is upset, and it's a surprise when he says, 'I think I'm starting to become like him."'

Advice On Writing

"Do a lot of it, and don't expect to do it perfectly the first time. Have fun with it. That's why we do it."

And Now a Word from Our Sponsor . . .

Since we're talking comedy here, let's talk about what's really the funniest stuff around—commercials! Fake commercials are a great way to begin and end your sitcoms, or you can just act them out for fun! Try this script for a new, improved product called Vampire–Off. Then make up your own commercials. Don't worry if they're dumb—they can't possibly be worse than the ones on TV!

Vampire–Off Commercial

The Cast

- Announcer
- Vampire
- Neighbor

Props

- an empty cereal box
- a piece of blank paper
- glue or tape
- some garlic
- crayons or felt-tip markers
- talcum powder
- measuring cup
- small boxes to be used as "Vampire Motels" (traps) els
- a spray bottle full of water
- a black cape
- vampire teeth
- a table

The Setup

Glue or tape the blank piece of paper to the front of the cereal box. Write "Vampire-Off" on

it in big letters. Draw a picture of garlic on the paper if you want. Put the garlic inside the box.

Put the black cape and vampire teeth on the person playing the vampire.

Put the cereal box, talcum powder, sprayer, and small boxes on the table.

The Script

Announcer: Vampires can be such a pesky household problem.

THE VAMPIRE ENTERS.

Announcer: Vampires came in and we couldn't get rid of them. We tried everything! Powders didn't work.

THE ANNOUNCER THROWS POWDER AT THE VAMPIRE. THE VAMPIRE KEEPS COMING CLOSER.

Announcer: Sprays didn't work.

THE ANNOUNCER SQUIRTS WATER AT THE VAMPIRE WITH THE WATER SPRAYER. THE VAMPIRE KEEPS COMING CLOSER.

Announcer: Even Vampire Motels were useless.

THE ANNOUNCER PUTS THE "VAMPIRE MOTELS" ON THE FLOOR. THE VAMPIRE STEPS ON THEM AND COMES CLOSER.

Announcer: Then we tried Vampire-Off. It's loaded with garlic!

THE ANNOUNCER PICKS UP THE BOX OF VAMPIRE–OFF, REACHES IN, AND TAKES OUT A CLOVE OF GARLIC. HE/SHE PRETENDS TO EAT IT, THEN BREATHES ON THE APPROACHING VAMPIRE. THE VAMPIRE COVERS HIS OR HER OWN FACE AND RUNS AWAY.

Announcer: See? Works like a charm.

THE DOORBELL RINGS (SOMEONE CAN JUST SAY "DING DONG"). THE ANNOUNCER GOES TO A PRETEND DOOR AND OPENS IT. THERE STANDS A NEIGHBOR, HOLDING A MEASURING CUP.

Neighbor: Hi there, neighbor! May I borrow a cup of sugar?

Announcer (breathing heavily on the neighbor): Hiiiiii! Sure.

THE NEIGHBOR SCREAMS AND RUNS AWAY.

Announcer: It's great for getting rid of neighbors, too!

THE ANNOUNCER HOLDS THE BOX OF VAMPIRE-OFF NEXT TO HIS OR HER FACE. THE VAMPIRE SPEAKS FROM OFFSTAGE, AS IF IN A VOICE-OVER.

Vampire: Vampire-Off gets rid of vampires— and everybody else!

THE END

Rubber Chicken Commercial

Props

- a rubber chicken (if you can't get a rubber chicken, use a stuffed animal and change the words "rubber chicken" in the script to the name of the animal)
- kitchen table
- enough glasses, plates, food, etc. for four place settings for dinner
- serving platter
- cardboard or toy microphone for announcer

The Cast

- Father
- Mother
- Son
- Daughter
- Announcer

The Setup

Set the four places at the table and arrange the family around it. Place the rubber chicken on the platter, and put the platter in the center of the table. The announcer stands off to the side and speaks into the microphone.

The Script

Announcer (IN LOUD WHISPER): We've secretly replaced Mrs. Singer's roast chicken with a disgusting rubber chicken. Let's see if anyone in the family notices.. . .

Son: Yuck! Chicken again? Why can't we have something good—like Pop-Tarts or Ho Ho's?

Father: Put a lid on it, son. We had Pop-Tarts and Ho Ho's for dinner last night and the night before. We can't have vegetarian meals *every* night!

Daughter: But Mom's chicken is always so *tough!* Last time I took a bite, it bit me back!

Mother: I cut the head off this time, dear—so it can't bite you tonight. (TO HUSBAND) You don't think my chicken is tough, do you?

Father: Of course not—ha ha! I'm just using this hatchet and sledgehammer on it because they're *faster* than a knife!

Son (TASTING FROM HIS PLATE): Yummm! Mom, this chicken is *great!*

Mother: Put that down, son. That's not my chicken. You got the dog's dish by mistake!

Son (HOLDING A HAND OVER HIS MOUTH): GAAAAACK!

Announcer (IN LOUD WHISPER): The Singers are about to bite into the rubber chicken.

Son (POINTING AT ANNOUNCER): Hey, who's he?

Announcer (IGNORING SON): Let's see if anyone notices what we've done.. . .

Father: Yummm! Delicious!

Daughter: Yeah, Mom, this chicken is great. The *best!*

Son: Wow! You should make this chicken for dinner *every* night!

Mother (VERY ANGRILY): *You Pigs!!* (SHE PICKS UP THE RUBBER CHICKEN BY THE FEET AND BEGINS SWINGING IT FURIOUSLY, HITTING THE TABLE WITH IT.) This isn't my chicken! It's rubber! A rubber chicken! How *dare* you!!

Father (BEING HIT DESPITE DUCKING & DODGING): Stop! Stop! Why'd you switch chickens?

Mother: I *knew* none of you had any taste at all! I'm never cooking again! From now on, we go *out* for dinner every night!

MOTHER THEN KEEPS BASHING THE TABLE ANGRILY WITH THE RUBBER CHICKEN, AS THE ANNOUNCER STEPS FORWARD.

Announcer: This has been a public service announcement from the National Restaurant Association. Why risk dinnertime violence? Go out for dinner—*every* night!

Mother (ANGRILY, TO ANNOUNCER): *You* shut up, too!

SHE GOES AFTER THE ANNOUNCER, SWINGING THE RUBBER CHICKEN, AND CHASES THE ANNOUNCER OFFSTAGE.

THE END

7

Your Neighborhood's Craziest Home Videos

- The first time your sister tried to walk in high heels.
- The time your baby brother's diaper fell off in front of all your friends!
- The day you put too much soap in the dishwasher and the whole kitchen filled with bubbles!

Your friends, relatives, and neighbors are the stars when you make your own funny home videos.

No matter where you live, there's a show in every neighborhood, and it's just waiting for someone like you with real Nickelodeon know-how to produce it.

For Your Neighborhood's Craziest Home Videos you don't have to hire celebrities or actors. You don't have to write a script. And there are no rehearsals. Your neighborhood's home video show stars your friends and families, doing what they do every day but doing it on tape. You do, however, need a video camera—and permission to use it. If you don't have a camera, maybe you can borrow one from a friend or from school. If your family has a camera but you're not allowed to use it, that's no big problem. Just get someone who can use it to work with you. That person can handle the equipment while you produce and direct. (That means you get to tell the camera person what to do.)

There are two kinds of really funny home videos: Instant Yuks, funny things that just happen that you manage to get on tape, and HidVids, funny videos that you make happen and tape secretly.

Instant Yuks

Instant Yuks can happen anywhere: at lunch, in the backyard, at your cousin's birthday party—anywhere.

Instant Yuksters have to carry their video cameras and be ready, at a moment's notice, to raise the eyepiece to their eye and push the record button. One slip, one case of bad timing, and it's gone. When it comes to Instant Yuks, there are no instant replays.

Instant Yuksters have to sense when something funny could happen. When your mother says, "Going to wallpaper the bedroom!" take that video camera and follow her. When your friend says, "I've never tried skateboarding but it doesn't look too hard," keep your viewfinder trained in his or her direction. When your sister decides to give the dog a bath, don't be too far off with the equipment.

Instant Yuk Sampler

Keep your eyes open for good instant Yuk possibilities like these:
- People unwrapping presents can be funny. Catch their expressions of surprise—or is it shock?
- If you see a baby around food, grab your camcorder. Something funny or messy or both is going to happen.
- People learning to do something, like skating, can be pretty funny.

- Watch your pets. Do they make funny movements when they sleep? Do they have weird habits?
- People getting into a cold swimming pool ...You get the idea.

HidVids

"HidVid" stands for "Hidden Video." When it comes to HidVids, you're in charge. HidVids are set up by you in advance and taped by you in secret. They take brains, imagination, and split-second timing. HidVids need a plan of action, a joke, a keen eye, and the ability to keep a straight face.

A HidVid puts a person in a situation and then tapes the reaction. HidVids shouldn't be mean, or they won't be very funny. But the best ones are, well, a little embarrassing.

HidVid Sampler

Put your camera on a tripod and turn it on to the autofocus setting. That way you can record without being in the room. Or else you can get someone to hide and work the camera while you set things rolling. But you don't have to be all that sneaky. Most people won't notice that the camera is on and that you're taping.

Try these funny setups:

• Hide a rubber mouse in the refrigerator, behind the milk. Get set to tape your family's reaction at breakfast time.

• Put some sour milk or smelly cheese or other nasty-smelling stuff in or behind a vase of flowers. Tape people's reactions as they sniff the flowers and get a shock.

• Give a friend an ice-cream cone with a hole in the bottom. Then leave the room, having made sure there are no napkins or paper towels around. Tape what the friend does as the ice cream gets really melty and messy.

• When no one is around, put green food coloring in your family's milk. Put the container back in the refrigerator. Then videotape your family's reactions when they pour out a glass. (This can be even funnier if you insist there's absolutely nothing weird about the milk and drink a big glass of it.)

Putting It All Together

What good is all this embarrassing material if you don't have an audience to show it to? Call a meeting of the kids in your neighborhood. Tell them you want to put on Your Neighborhood's Craziest Home Videos. Tell them to make their own HidVids, Instant Yuks, music videos, sitcoms, funny commercials, and skits. Then pick a day and put on your show. You can sell tickets or just invite family and friends.

After the show is over, have your audience vote on which was the funniest. Then give the winner a prize.